the things I didn't say in therapy

Logan Duane

the things I didn't say in therapy

Instagram
@logan.duane.poetry

Copyright © 2020 Logan Reardon

To request permissions, contact the publisher at
loganduanepoetry@gmail.com

the things I didn't say in therapy

For Karen Girvan

the woman who believed
in me,
walked with me through
this journey,
taught me the power of
my words,
and gave me the strength
to write.

For my baby girl, Tori

the dog who saved
my life,
and showed me what
it's like
to truly love.

May you both rest
as peacefully as
you lived.

Contents:

about grief and sadness

trigger warning: death, suicide & depression

the things I didn't say in therapy

My words growled from the pit of my stomach
like an angry wolf
ready to feast upon
what was left of my quivering soul.

"How are you feeling today?"
she asked from the cozy chair across the room.

With dead, lifeless eyes
holding back the animal inside of me
I said

"I'm great."

-[the things I didn't say in therapy]

the things I didn't say in therapy

I'm the kind of sad that
makes me feel like
I will never find the sun again.

the things I didn't say in therapy

It was 2:34 a.m.
You spoke softly through the phone
and told me that I would be okay.
Your comforting words wrapped around me
and hugged me tightly
like my favorite blanket.

"He can not hurt you anymore."

the things I didn't say in therapy

It's 2:34 a.m.,
and instead of sleeping
I'm trying to find the words
to explain how the world looks
without you in it.

-[you took the sun with you]

the things I didn't say in therapy

Remembering you tastes like
whiskey on the rocks -
it burns like hell going down
but the buzz is too addicting
to put down the glass.

the things I didn't say in therapy

The icy grip of death
coiled around your neck
like a snake with its
beloved prey.

You kissed away tears from my cheeks
and promised
"Don't worry,
I'll be okay."

My chest grew heavy;
burdened with all of the words
that I didn't have time
to say.

As your last breath
escaped from your lips
a dark, morose cloud surrounded me
and threatened to forever stay.

I wept.

...it wasn't supposed to end that way.

...it was never supposed to end that way.

the things I didn't say in therapy

Are there sunflowers
where you are?

-*[questions from your graveside]*

the things I didn't say in therapy

I sat close to you as I read
the last passages from
Of Mice and Men
and swore that nothing would ever
break my heart
like the ending of that novella.

On the day that you died
I held the copy that you gave me
right up against my beating chest
and watched as
depression laden tears stained its pages.

My heart shattered between every word.

the things I didn't say in therapy

Do not fucking tell me that
"they're in a better place"
when they belong here with me.

-[selfish cries]

the things I didn't say in therapy

I don't want to eat
I can't sleep
My shampoo bottle has gone dry waiting for me to
use it
My heart has withdrawn so deeply into my body
that I can't hear it crying out for you anymore
I don't know what day it is
what time it is
hell, I don't even know where I am
I've never known pain like this
A pain that only you would know how to fix
A pain that echoes in my head so loudly
that my ears ring
and I can't hear them telling me to
get out of bed
I've forgotten how to write
My mouth is sealed tightly
bound by a deep, burning depression
that melts my lips together
I can't breathe
I don't want to
The air is too heavy
for my lungs

the things I didn't say in therapy

You came to me
in the shadows of my nightmares
and reminded me that
my memories of you
die with me.

-*[suicide prevention]*

the things I didn't say in therapy

I've begged and pleaded
to not wake up.
I've prayed
to a God that I don't believe in
to let me slip away in the night
as I sleep.
For years
I wished on shooting starts
to not live to see another moon.

But, here I sit
writing this shit

as your beautiful,
kind heart
lays six feet underground.
A person so vibrant and full of life
just gone

and I think it's supposed to make me
feel grateful
for the breath that I hold in my lungs

but I will hold this breath
until I am blue in the face
because it's supposed to belong to you -
not me.

the things I didn't say in therapy

"I guess I'm so
angry
because everyone around me
expects me to just fucking move on
when every last piece of my heart
died with her."

-*[today I cried in therapy]*

the things I didn't say in therapy

My heart aches.

Not like the ache you feel
between your eyes
when you forget to wear your glasses,
or the ache in your tooth
when you have a cavity.

My heart aches like
there's one million hands
tearing at its most tender parts.
Like there's a raging fire
burning in its deepest pits,
as if it might pour out of my chest
like the tears from my eyes.

My heart aches
because I miss you.

the things I didn't say in therapy

If time is supposed to
heal all wounds,
then why is
the poetry harder to write
and the days harder to fight
with each *tick* of the clock that passes?

the things I didn't say in therapy

I'm not quite sure what day it is;
I don't even know where I am.
I'm just a wandering shell of flesh and bones
lost in a world
where I can no longer hold your hand.

the things I didn't say in therapy

Sadness poured from my fingertips
as I slid them along your sweet, sweet face
for the final time.

the things I didn't say in therapy

Death
makes a year
feel like just yesterday,
because the pain still stings
in the exact same way.

-[*missing you today*]

the things I didn't say in therapy

I would sell my soul to the devil
if she would allow me
one more moment
with you.

the things I didn't say in therapy

"And know that there are people in your life
who care about you,
and want the best for you. I hope you know I'm one
of them."

"Do you ever stop and listen to yourself?
I am so
damned proud of you."

-[the last I heard from you]

the things I didn't say in therapy

I stopped believing in God
after endless nights of
praying
and begging
for him to take my soul from my body
so I couldn't feel the pain
anymore.

the things I didn't say in therapy

Tell me,
what am I supposed to do
when I reach the end of my
list of coping mechanisms
and still wish myself dead?

-*[the things they don't tell you in therapy]*

the things I didn't say in therapy

Please give me some time
and space.
I never thought I would survive this long;
I have no idea
what I'm doing
or what I really want for myself.

Please have patience with me.
I never got to plan
for my adult life.

the things I didn't say in therapy

I died 1,000 times
to save you only once,

just to have you turn around
and spit
into my grave.

the things I didn't say in therapy

They always tell you that
suicide is not the answer,
but never actually tell you
what the answer is.

the things I didn't say in therapy

It's so dark in here tonight
and I simply can not figure out
how to make it bright
again.
Have I always been so dreary,
or has the pain of you
returned to my brain?

the things I didn't say in therapy

A passionate, burning anger
resides deep inside of me;
so powerful that I feel
frightened,
because I don't know why it's there
and I don't know how to
put out it's flames.

the things I didn't say in therapy

Even in death,
I can still feel
how much you love me,

and it keeps me alive.

the things I didn't say in therapy

Each time you come to me in my dreams
I am reminded that
you gave me the strength and skills
to keep going without you here.

-*[therapy dogs never die]*

about pain & abuse

trigger warning: sexual assault & abuse

the things I didn't say in therapy

How loud do I have to scream
for someone to finally
hear my story?

the things I didn't say in therapy

I'm so tired of screaming,

but it's the only thing that gets you to
shut the fuck up
and listen to me.

the things I didn't say in therapy

I watched silently as
your love for me
became
your lust
for my body.

the things I didn't say in therapy

I watched silently as
your love for me
faded more and more
each time I said
"no."

the things I didn't say in therapy

I experienced heartbreak for the first time
at a very young age
when I realized that there is
so much injustice
and pain around me.
It hurt so deeply to know
that it wasn't
just me.

the things I didn't say in therapy

I stared blankly into my mirror
at the body that was once mine.

Lifeless tears rolled down my face
as marks from the hands of others
stained my skin,
claiming me as their own.

the things I didn't say in therapy

There aren't enough words in the english language
to explain how it feels to be
hunted.

I'm too afraid to
leave my house.

Paranoia has convinced me that
I can smell you waiting for me
from among the ditches that
line my driveway.

I can feel you stalking me
like a wolf in the wild
waiting for the perfect chance
to rip the flesh
from an unsuspecting deer.

But, I'm not a deer,
I'm a woman.

And you're not a wolf,
you're a man.

This isn't some
primitive instinct that you can't control.

the things I didn't say in therapy

You're a human predator

with a lust for
innocent girls.

the things I didn't say in therapy

I never know when
the panic will set it, but
when it does,
even my own reflection
threatens to consume me.

the things I didn't say in therapy

I preach that
all bodies are beautiful,
but I can't even look at mine
without crying.

-[hypocrisy]

the things I didn't say in therapy

To look at yourself in the mirror
and want to die
is a feeling that can can not be described to those
that have never existed in such
darkness.

the things I didn't say in therapy

You confused
sex
with love.

the things I didn't say in therapy

I wear a scarlet "w" on my chest
as a constant reminder that
I am your Hester Prynne,
nothing more that the
dirty little whore
you victimized.

the things I didn't say in therapy

"I love you,"
you say,

but the words bleed from your lips
as you struggle to look me in the eyes.

"I love you,"
you say,

but your hands tremble beneath
the weight of the lies you hold in your
sweaty palms.

"I love you, too,"

I whisper to you from beneath
the safety of this blanket,

hoping that you can't hear me
cry.

the things I didn't say in therapy

In a desperate cry for love and affection,
I allowed you to take residency
between my legs.

the things I didn't say in therapy

The part that no one talks about is how much it hurts
to have sex for the rest of your life. It's like the
memories of you rip apart my vagina, long after you
took that space from me. It's a never ending cycle of
dying to be touched by someone else, and cowering
in fear at even the most delicate fingertips. I hate you
for using my body for your sick, twisted pleasure. I
hate you for lingering here where you don't belong. I
hate everyone that took your side as I cried out on my
knees begging for someone, anyone, to make the pain
stop. The Red Sea ran from between my legs while
people fed you sympathy on a silver fucking platter.
People that I once called friends fell for the
manipulative lies that spilled from your blackened
lips. I hate you for what you have done to me; and if
you ever thought that I would sit in the corner with
stitches sealing my lips, you were so fucking wrong.

the things I didn't say in therapy

My bedroom fell silent
as my tired, naked body
stood before my bleak reflection.

Every word you said about
love
and respect
poured out from within
my aching chest
with each beat of my broken heart.

On my knees
I wept.
Your lies dripped from my eyes
in an endless storm of
concrete rainfall
that crashed to the floor.

-[pathological liar]

the things I didn't say in therapy

I find myself hopelessly dreaming
of rooting my feet
into the soft earth below me,
and giving gentle kisses to the bees
as they say hello.
I find myself longing
to let my body
sway in the wind,
and carelessly dance with the trees.
I ache for my mirror to show me
the flower
that I've always wanted to be -
but instead it always shatters into
a million broken pieces on the bathroom floor,
threatening to rip open my heart
again.

the things I didn't say in therapy

How does it feel to know
that a mere child
tried to take her own life
because of the hate that you spit
from your mouth?

the things I didn't say in therapy

When a caged animal strikes,
we blame it on the
inhumane conditions
that it was forced to live in.

When a caged woman strikes,
we blame it on
insanity,
or her eagerness to open her legs.

-[if lions were whores]

"You deserved it."
"No one is going to believe you."
"That's not rape."
"You're a lying whore."
"But, you always want sex."
"You're just looking for attention."
"You're just seeking revenge."

"Stop lying."
"Stop lying."
"Stop lying."

-[the things I've heard]

the things I didn't say in therapy

I came to you
with my heart
bleeding from within,
aching and screaming to be held
by hands that weren't his

and you slammed the door in my face.

the things I didn't say in therapy

Tell me how the fuck you sleep at night
with a heart so full
of selfish, backstabbing bullshit.

the things I didn't say in therapy

You ripped the lungs from my chest
and expected me
to breathe for you.

the things I didn't say in therapy

I never thought I would see the day
where we had to say goodbye.
What happened to the
passionate and
intimate love
that our hearts once knew so well?
How did two souls
intertwined in each other
travel galaxies apart,
without noticing that the stars
were shining differently?

You've changed
I've changed

and I can't decide if it's for better
or for worse.
What used to make me feel so safe
now makes me fearful
to return to the place I'm supposed to call home.

I can't live in fear anymore
and you can't take the pain anymore

so with tears in my eyes

the things I didn't say in therapy

I will kiss you one last time
and watch
as the person I confused as my soulmate
silently walks away.

the things I didn't say in therapy

I'm angry
because you only hear what I have to say
in my nightmares.

the things I didn't say in therapy

The bad in you outweighed the good.
But, no matter what you did
I defended you
like my life depended on it

as you held a gun to the back of my head.

the things I didn't say in therapy

The problem with you and I
is that there is no you and I.

There's you,
and there's me.

Two lovers so full of
rage and regret
that their hearts can't hold any
forgiveness and love.
Two souls, light-years apart
in a universe where they once held hands.

Where did you go?
What have we become?

Oceans of emptiness fill the space between us
and I'm worried that I might
drown
if I try to make my way
back to you.

the things I didn't say in therapy

I loved you more yesterday
than I do today
and I'm pretty sure
it's not supposed to be that way.

the things I didn't say in therapy

I just want to know what it's like
to breathe
without feeling like
my lungs might collapse
under the pressure from what it takes
to be perfect for you.

the things I didn't say in therapy

I hope you choke
on the lies you spread about me.

the things I didn't say in therapy

Your lips caressed my ear and you whispered
"I love you"
in the darkness of your room.
You fucked me under the blanket of stars
that peered into
the open window.
In the tender hours of the morning
I rolled over to kiss you awake
and found nothing but emptiness beside me
in your bed

and just like the night
you came and left,
never to be felt again.

the things I didn't say in therapy

I wanted you to be the one
so badly that
I painted a picture of you in my mind
that showed me a person who
didn't exist.

the things I didn't say in therapy

For once I want to be
a person that isn't
so easily replaced.

the things I didn't say in therapy

I have found myself
stuck
in a never ending cycle
of hating the way that I am
and not knowing how to fix it -

and I want you to know that
I'm sorry
for being this way.

about love

the things I didn't say in therapy

Those golden eyes
caught my attention from across the room
and I knew
that I was going to get into
a whole lot of trouble with you.

the things I didn't say in therapy

You are what happens when
the sunshine
makes love with a sweet summer meadow;
a love child of
vibrant light
and delicate euphoria.

the things I didn't say in therapy

I want to know what it's like
to wander into your soul.
Would I need a map?
Or, would your heart be my compass -
gently guiding me to your
most delicate secrets?

I want to know them all.

the things I didn't say in therapy

I would light myself on fire
just to bring you
warmth.

the things I didn't say in therapy

Your lips brushed my neck
like a paintbrush crafting delicate art.
Miles and miles of mountains
arose as goosebumps on my skin
with each intoxicating touch.
Thunder crashed between my inner thighs
as our bodies collided into one.
One body. One soul. One mind.

As each moment passed
you convinced me that nothing was more precious
than soul mates making love.

the things I didn't say in therapy

"You mend broken hearts
even when yours is
shattered to pieces.
You carry the burdens of others
when you don't have the strength
to carry yourself.
So many bad things have happened to you
in this life,
but none of it could ever taint
the purest and
most beautiful soul
I've ever seen."

-[how was I not supposed to fall in love with you?]

the things I didn't say in therapy

"You look like sunshine,"
he said
as I rolled over to meet his gaze
with morning breath
and bed head.

I smiled, because
for the very first time,
I actually believed him.

the things I didn't say in therapy

You are the match
that ignites my demons into flames.
You are my protector,
guarding my soul from
the ghosts
that haunt my mind.

-[I need you]

the things I didn't say in therapy

Please forgive me
if I am
speechless
as your captivating soul
dances along the walls of my heart,
threatening to capture it
and keep it locked forever.

the things I didn't say in therapy

Black holes for hearts
Love dripping in soft tears
Lustful stares disguised as devotion

Not with you.

Gentle hands touch my
mind
soul
body
like only you can,
because when two lovers collide
every living creature on Mother Earth
can feel the fire as their bodies
melt into one
graceful goddess.

You give me wings.

With each kiss I swear
I fly closer to touching
the edge of the universe,
lost among the stars
that shine when we tangle up
in each other.

the things I didn't say in therapy

I don't mind being lost
as long as

I have you
to lead me back to the home
that I have found within our love.

the things I didn't say in therapy

Today, you made me
avocado toast in bed,
gave me delicate forehead kisses,
wrapped your arms around me and said
"I will cherish you forever."

You give me a reason to
appreciate
waking up in the morning.

the things I didn't say in therapy

You and I have the kind of love story
that I have always dreamed of.
The
"drop everything in the night and leave together"
kind of love story.
The
"kissing in public because we can't wait any longer"
kind of love story.
The
"run away on a random rainy day and get married"
kind of love story.
The
"I will love you forever"
kind of love story,
that everyone should be lucky enough to experience.

the things I didn't say in therapy

Darling,
let's watch the world burn.
Let's light
raging, ghastly fires
that erupt with each sound
that escapes your lips.
Let's run through the streets and
open up our mouths to let
ashes
fall to the tips of our tongues
like snowflakes.
Let's share a kiss
and watch as people stop and stare,
because our love burns brighter
than the flames that surround us.
I want to turn this town into
a beautiful wasteland
with you.

the things I didn't say in therapy

Every minute
of every hour
of every day

I will never get
enough of you.

the things I didn't say in therapy

Fear
(or maybe fearlessness)
rings violently in my ears
as the sound of your tender voice
beats on their drums,
like the most elegant matching band
the whole world has ever heard.

Sadness
(or is it relief)
for a love bleeding in my hands
that I ever so desperately cling to.
Please hold me
as we watch it take its last breath
together.

Merely sex
(a blissful dance between your sheets)
Legs tangled in a spider web
of beautiful infidelity;
ignited by fires of
cautious passion and desire.

the things I didn't say in therapy

Lust
(genuine love)
whispers for you between my legs.
My unforetold fantasies drip from
your lips
as your telling eyes meet mine
from my inner thighs.

Spinning
(the world stops when I'm with you)
flying around in erratic circles
like I may never come down,
but as you grace my skin with your
intoxicating touch,
all the chaos makes perfect sense.

the things I didn't say in therapy

Your soul is the glue
that mended my shattered remains;
it weaved through pieces of me
and brought me back to life.
Your heart wrote a story
on my tattered skin;
it spoke of love without limits
and endless happy days.

the things I didn't say in therapy

I love you
like the moon
loves the tides
and the stars
love the skies.

-[galaxies of love for you]

the things I didn't say in therapy

Did you know
that your eyes become
oceans
when they lock into mine?
Wave after wave
you crash into the shores of my heart,
threatening to carry me away
with each delicate blink.

Did you know
that your hands ignite
fires
that dance along my body
and leave every inch of skin
begging to be burned by you?

Did you know
that your lips plant
gardens
with each tender kiss
left on my hands that you hold?
Baby, we make beautiful flowers.

the things I didn't say in therapy

Did you know
that your words
thrived
in the deepest part of my soul
and made me fall in love?

the things I didn't say in therapy

He was my escape
from a world that kept me
trapped.

-[claustrophobia]

the things I didn't say in therapy

With feet rooted beneath the earth,
you grabbed me by the hands
and showed me how to bloom.

-*[blooming with you]*

the things I didn't say in therapy

Love
comes to us
in the
strangest ways.

the things I didn't say in therapy

How strange it is
to love someone
that you've never met.

the things I didn't say in therapy

There are so many words in a day
that I forget to say to you in the midst
of life's hustle and bustle.
Like
"My life with you makes all of my
pain
worth something",
or
"each time you smile,
broken pieces of me
melt back together."

But, there is really one thing
that I that I vow to never forget to shout
from the tops of the highest mountains
with each day that passes -

"You'll be the world's best dad."

the things I didn't say in therapy

My eyes fill up with tears
as I watched you press your lips
on my delicate skin;
certain that our son's innocent cheeks
rested just below the surface.

the things I didn't say in therapy

My son
did not strip me of my youth,
ruin my plans,
or dampen my quality of life.

There is nothing that I want to experience
without him.

about recovery

the things I didn't say in therapy

I refuse to feel ashamed
of the story stained on my heart.

the things I didn't say in therapy

The hardest part of growing up
is learning how to do
what is best for you
without shame or guilt.

the things I didn't say in therapy

Today, I read somewhere that
every seven years,
your body has replaced
every
single
cell
with a brand new one.
A whole new body -
one that you have never seen,
one that you have never touched,
one that you will never have the opportunity to
tarnish.

Freedom.

the things I didn't say in therapy

I told myself that
I would be the bigger person,
and I will be...

...right after I say
fuck you
one last time.

the things I didn't say in therapy

I didn't want to write a poem about
the endless abuse you made me endure,
because I feared your backlash.

Then I realized that
I never mention your name
in my writing,

so the only way you can be angry with me
is to admit
what you've done.

the things I didn't say in therapy

I refuse to allow myself
to be hurt
by those who have never
truly loved me.

-[putting myself first]

the things I didn't say in therapy

You are no supporter of mine
if you also support the men
who assaulted me.

-*[betrayal]*

the things I didn't say in therapy

Thank you for showing me
that the words of others
don't define my character.

Thank you for allowing me
to experience toxicity,
so I know the difference between
you
and love.

Thank you for tearing me down,
and giving me the opportunity
to build myself back up.

Thank you for belittling me,
and forcing me to
believe in myself
when no one else did.

Lastly,

thank you for reading this
and knowing it's about you.

the things I didn't say in therapy

I don't regret being with you.

I regret allowing myself
to take the blame for the things
that you did to me.

the things I didn't say in therapy

Like a temporary tattoo
I washed you away from
my body.

My skin turned red and blotchy,
but at least I'm not
reminded of you
anymore.

the things I didn't say in therapy

I hope that she captures your heart
and earns your trust,
only so that she can
chew you up
and spit you out,
just like you did to me.

Find someone that
appreciates your touch,
but doesn't expect your body.

the things I didn't say in therapy

I hope she never knows the pain
you put me through.
I hope she never meets the monster
that I once knew.
I hope she realizes her self worth
before you do.

the things I didn't say in therapy

If you're reading this,
just know that
I'm done.
My neck encased in the grips of your
pernicious words,
struggling to breathe between
"worthless"
and "ugly."
No more.
Silent screams
beneath the gentle touch of
my favorite blanket -
it used to keep me safe.
No more.
Kisses from
streams of tears
rolling down my blushed cheeks -
they spell out your name.
No more.
The left and right sides of my brain
cling to each other,
on their knees begging for
the undying pain to stop.
No more.

If you're reading this,
just know that

the things I didn't say in therapy

I'm done

giving you this power.

-[a letter to my abuser]

the things I didn't say in therapy

No matter how many times you
kick me down,
I will bloom
stronger
in the spring.

the things I didn't say in therapy

I refuse to measure my self worth
by the number of people
I've had sex with,

consentual or not.

-*[sex(ual trauma) does not define me]*

the things I didn't say in therapy

The concept of virginity is
just another tool used
by society
to keep women in their place.

It's as if our bodies are
delicate little flowers
patented by religion
and powerful men.

It's as if our bodies
are not our own
until someone has
sex with it.

-*[deflowered]*

the things I didn't say in therapy

Please,
say what you want about me.
Tell them that I'm
nothing more than a
useless whore.
Tell them I'm a
washed up bitch
that stained the purity of your name.
Erase my face from
the pages of your memories
like the mistake you
make me out to be.
Spit my name
into the Devil's gaping mouth
and allow her to swallow me whole.

Please,
do whatever the fuck
helps you sleep at night.
Meanwhile,

I'll be raising my son
to be twice the man
that you are.

the things I didn't say in therapy

Never underestimate the power
of a woman.

the things I didn't say in therapy

I'm so fucking tired of
feeling this angry

so I guess it's time
I erase you from
every corner
of my mind.

the things I didn't say in therapy

I have found that
the hardest time to walk away
is when you have nothing left
to hold onto.

-*[why is it so hard to let go?]*

the things I didn't say in therapy

I allow my fingertips to trace
each mark on my skin,
like tiny roadmaps
that outline all the places I've been.

From the valleys of
rock bottom,
to the sun kissed tips of the very top,
each scar reminds me that
no one but me
gets to choose where I go next.

the things I didn't say in therapy

Stop.

Stop trying to save the world,
and start trying to save yourself.

-*[sometimes, the world does revolve around you]*

the things I didn't say in therapy

I vow to never force my son
to grow up too fast.

-*[innocence is only found in childhood]*

the things I didn't say in therapy

When I started dating women,
I vowed to always treat them
far better than any man
had ever treated me.

And when I started dating men,
I vowed to always show them
what a woman
is worth.

-[the beauty in her petals]

the things I didn't say in therapy

Woman,
man,
child,
anyone in between,

no one has the right to your body
without your permission.

-*[assault does not discriminate]*

the things I didn't say in therapy

I wish I could offer you more than
a washed up college drop out
left lost,
confused,
and unsure,
with nothing more to show for herself
other than a notepad and pen.

I'm sorry I wasted so much time
chasing everything except for
my dreams
(whatever those are).

I'm not sure where I'm going.
I barely know how I'll get through this week.

Despite all of this,
I am positive of one thing.

I will work everyday for the rest of my life
to make sure
that you have the greatest mom,
the greatest life,
and everything you could ever dream of
for as long as I live.

-*[a letter to my unborn son]*

the things I didn't say in therapy

The more you grow,
little one,
the bigger I become

and the more I learn
to love what my body
is capable of.

the things I didn't say in therapy

Every pitter patter
of your tiny feet
along the walls if my stomach
reminds me why

I'm alive.

the things I didn't say in therapy

The day that you are finally born
will be the first day
of my life.

the things I didn't say in therapy

I wish you knew
how proud of you I am.

I wish you knew
how lucky I feel
to have shared my life with you.

-[a letter to my siblings]

the things I didn't say in therapy

My wish for you is that
you never find yourself with someone
that makes you feel like
you're hard to love.

the things I didn't say in therapy

I'm not searching for answers
in you anymore.

the things I didn't say in therapy

I've given up on the girl
I thought I had to be,
and instead I choose to embrace the girl
that I have kept hidden for so long.

I've planted my insecurities like flowers,
allowing them to flourish and bloom.

I've silenced the voices in my head
that don't come from a place of
self love and forgiveness.

the things I didn't say in therapy

One day,
I will have the courage to
put my writing
my story
out there.
One day,
the truth will prevail
over your cacophony of lies.

the things I didn't say in therapy

I wish not for revenge,

only justice.

the things I didn't say in therapy

You have done nothing to warrant the pain that
you're feeling. You did nothing to deserve what
you've gone through. No matter how many times
your brain tries to convince you that you don't belong
here on this earth, it's wrong. Your life matters. Your
happiness matters. You deserve to sit in a field of
your favorite flowers and flip through the pages of a
treasured book. You deserve to wake up in the
morning and smile at the sun as it tenderly kisses
your sleepy cheeks. No one gets to take away your
joy. No one gets to take away your core values and
beliefs. You are strong. You are brave. You're allowed
to wear confidence on your shoulders like a badge of
honor. You're allowed to take up space with your
body and your words without feeling guilty. You're
not a burden. You matter. You matter. You matter.

-*[positive affirmations]*

the things I didn't say in therapy

I like to believe that
you've become the biggest,
most beautiful sunflower
of them all.

-[I left one by your graveside]

the things I didn't say in therapy

"I'm tired of only ever seeing
rain
when I look outside my windows.
I think it's time I start
searching for the sun."

-[breakthroughs]

the things I didn't say in therapy

"Your recovery will never be
a single uphill slope.
You will climb mountains,
fight fires,
tumble
and stand back up

but you will
stand back up

and you will
survive."

-[what I learned in therapy]

Made in the USA
Coppell, TX
29 November 2022

87248900R00083